# WRITINGS IN THE DUST

# Writings in the Dust

*Vivid Narratives of Some of the Bible's
Most Notable Characters*

## Carl E. Price

The Upper Room
Nashville, Tennessee

Writings in the Dust

The scripture quotations not otherwise identified are from the Revised Standard Version of the Bible, copyrighted 1946, 1952 and © 1971 by the Division of Christian Education, National Council of Churches of Christ in the United States of America, and are used by permission.

Any scripture quotation designated AP is the author's paraphrase.


Book Design: Harriette Bateman
Cover Design: Steve Laughbaum
First Printing: March 1984(7)
Library of Congress Catalog Card Number: 83-51397
ISBN: 0-8358-0474-7
Printed in the United States of America

TO
PAT,
*with whom I share a ministry*
*and a life*

# CONTENTS

WRITINGS IN THE DUST

# INTRODUCTION

The title of this book has a broader meaning in my own mind than the one story whose chapter heading it happens to be. *Writings in the Dust* is a reminder that time and again God has sought to express divine will, purpose, and intentions in the dust of the human lives of creation. The Bible begins with just such a thought. In the second chapter of Genesis we read:

> Then the Lord God formed man of dust from the ground and breathed into his nostrils the breath of life; and man became a living being.
>
> —Genesis 2:7

Writings in the dust! God once sought divine expression in the dust of our being. The Incarnation is the crowning example of what dust becomes when God enters fully into it.

For all the glory that Christ's exaltation of dust demonstrates, there are lesser examples that merit our study and reflection as well. Not that they teach us as fully as he can teach us, and not that we are to follow them

*11*

instead of Christ, but that even in the imperfect dust of other lives, we can see tracings of the hand of the Creator.

It is important in this kind of Bible study and meditation to remain faithful to the scripture that provides its base. While situations may lend themselves to elaboration and interpretation, it is critical not to let our imaginations replace the Bible. Storytelling is a powerful medium, and readers who are not very familiar with the Bible itself may recall our stories as if they were the scripture accounts. While we may elaborate and suggest details, the important part is to avoid contradiction or too fanciful exaggerations. The stories we weave should grow out of the pattern that scripture holds before us and the threads of the gospel should be clearly traced throughout the finished fabric.

In the preaching context, I have found a good, even enthusiastic reception to this style of sermon as a variation from the "usual." I think the story style opens the possibility of presenting ideas in a nonthreatening way that leaves the acceptance and response with the hearers, without the implication of an assumed verdict beforehand. Stories provide more of an opportunity for people to pursue the thoughts further in their own minds through the guidance of the Holy Spirit. Storytelling leaves final verdicts more open and suggested than challenged and demanded. While responses may not always be the desired goal, I am convinced that the approach reaches some who may erect defenses against a more direct approach.

Whether you read this book for personal Bible Study, for

preaching ideas, for devotions that you share with others, or simply because it looks interesting, I hope that it will help to fix certain passages and incidents in scripture more vividly in your mind by creating word pictures and emotional attitudes that reinforce the events upon which they are based. In some instances the background information or descriptions may give more meaning to the incident or provide a basis for a deeper understanding. Often the meaning of an event for our day can only be found when we enter into the time and circumstances of the day in which the event occurred and comprehend its meaning for that time, and then try to pull out of that meaning the meaning for our own time.

It is my earnest prayer that through these pages you will come to experience something of the events that are interpreted, not in the sense of improving your knowledge or adding to your information, but in the sense of entering into the situation and seeing with eyes of the Spirit the writings in the dust.

I am indebted to several people for this book. I would like to give credit to Frederick Speakman who several years ago wrote a book of narrative sermons and provided the initial incentive to do some of this style of writing. There has also been the encouragement of members of several congregations and fellow ministers who have offered words of encouragement when some of these chapters were presented as sermons, and they expressed the desire to have them in print. My gratitude goes to Buena Wilson, my secretary at First United Methodist Church in Midland, and to the volunteers she recruited to type these manuscripts for publication; and to my wife, Pat, who read and listened far more than a husband had a right to request, and offered encouragement and criticism that helped to make the finished product better than it would have been. Last, my thanks to Rueben Job, Janice Grana, and the staff at The Upper Room for their encouragement and help in getting these ideas into print.

Carl E. Price
*Midland, Michigan*
*June 13, 1983*

CHAPTER 1

# WITH OPEN HANDS

Genesis 22:1-14

Sarah sat in the shadowed shelter of the tent and wept. They were silent tears at the moment. A woman of her day knew that her husband's word was law. But his word could not stop her grief for what she feared was to come.

Abraham and their only son, Isaac, were vanishing specks in the distance, along with the two servants and the donkey that carried the large load of wood. They were evidently bound for the high country where no fuel would be found. Abraham had only said, "I go to sacrifice to the Most High." She tried to tell herself that her fears were unnecessary, that the two of them would soon return. The thoughts were unconvincing. She had spent too many nights listening to her husband's half-asleep rantings and sat through too many of his daytime murmurings at the religious practices of their neighbors to believe her hopes of a safe return to be anything but false hopes.

Last night had been the worst of all. He had tossed and

turned all night, and his nightmare dreams had been more vivid than ever. "I *do* love the Lord God as much as the Canaanites love their gods who are as nothing!" Then he would toss and turn some more, only to burst out again a short time later with some similar exclamation. Twice he had awakened himself with his ravings. She had known it would be a bad night when he came in from the herds and told her that another of the families near them had offered a child as a sacrifice to their god. Three times before he had heard such reports, and each time he would talk about how much he loved this God of the high places who had called him out of Haran and led them to Bethel and given him riches beyond dreams. Sarah did not doubt Abraham's devotion. She knew the courage it took to leave the comfortable, familiar lands of home. She had seen his bravery in battle. She knew his unselfish generosity to their nephew Lot. All were instances of his faith and devotion to the Most High, as he called this One who had no image or likeness as did the gods of those around them.

His faith had been far greater than hers when they were told in their old age that they would have a son! She remembered laughing. But then, she thought, she had had more grounds to doubt than he had! She was the one who had been unable to conceive through all the years when childbearing might have been expected of her. The problem had not been with Abraham. The birth of Ishmael to the handmaid Hagar who she had given him as wife proved that. No, she had no doubt of Abraham's great devotion.

*16*

In fact, it was knowing that devotion that caused her to sit in her tent and weep.

Sarah recognized that the practice of human sacrifice, as carried on by those around them, had become for Abraham a test of love. It sounded impossible, but there it was. Abraham had come to question his own faith. No one else was questioning it, but he was; and self is the most fearful interrogator of all. She had heard him say in one of his self-discussions to which she was present but not a party, "How can they love their gods so much? They are nothing compared to the Most High. Is their love greater than mine? I offer sheep and goats and cattle while they offer their children. How can they offer greater sacrifices to lesser gods?" So the thought had plagued him, day and night. It had become an obsession, a cancer in his mind, and today he had given way. The voice of God seemed to him to be speaking through his own questions.

Outside the tent Sarah could see the herds of cattle and camels and other livestock on the hills. She and Abraham were rich beyond belief, certainly beyond need. Why could he not offer a thousand sheep or a hundred oxen or. . . ? Then she knew why. It was because those things really meant so little. They owned so much that the usual sacrifices did not really cost them anything. People tended to measure gifts by their size or by the volume of the gift itself, but Sarah had come to know that *sacrifice* measured what was left as well as what was given. How then did you measure a gift out of abundance? Abraham could not

**17**

give out of poverty, so the measure of his devotion came to be the object that he loved the most. That was Isaac.

There were times when Sarah wondered if the anguish of soul and spirit wrapped up in ''that'' could be understood by anyone else. A son, in their culture, was more than bone of their bone, flesh of their flesh. A son was their posterity, the preservation of their name, their security in old age, their gift to the future, their immortality, their reason for life itself. Had they not been told that nations and kings would come from them? Were they not promised that the covenant of the Most High would be through their offspring? ''A father of many nations,'' God had called her husband. And it was all bound up in Isaac.

She feared that Abraham had not gone simply to offer his son, as awesome and unbelievable as that thought was; he had gone to offer everything that he lived for, dreamed of, hoped for—his future, his posterity, his hope of the covenant, his very self. He had gone to offer God everything that God had promised him. Abraham had gone to offer Isaac, and Sarah wept.

After a time that seemed an eternity, Sarah received them safely home again. She learned of the ram caught in the bushes and the voice calling Abraham to stay his hand. What began as a horrible story of human sacrifice ended up as a record that God does not want such actions.

I wonder if we can understand the challenge that confronted Abraham and apply it in any way to our own lives? Can we put ourselves in those harsh and bloody days when men and women struggled to understand the will and the word of God as it came to them in the unfolding revelation of who God is? Can we put ourselves in Abraham's time and culture and see events through his eyes, rather than judging him only by the light of nearly forty centuries?

We understand that God does not want the death of our children in worship. But given that we understand God does not want that kind of sacrifice, what does it mean to offer to God what Isaac symbolized to Abraham? Can we envision that? We are quick to reproach Abraham as an Old Testament fanatic who did not know the real heart of God. But can we approach his faith when it comes to laying all that Isaac represented upon the altar of sacrifice?

What about our hopes, our dreams, our ambitions, our aspirations, our possessions? What about *ourselves*? Suddenly the story is not academic anymore. It walks down our street and knocks on our door. God does still ask to be first in our lives, God does demand of us some measure of risk and sacrifice. Abraham was wrong in thinking that God wanted the death of Isaac, but Abraham was not wrong in recognizing that God's claim extends to all that we have and all that we are.

It is this element of sacrifice that has gone out of much of religion today. Faith is marketed as something for our benefit that makes no real demands upon us. Oh, there are a few requests now and then, but even those usually come with the promise of an excellent return on the investment. So we package faith as pop psychology that will earn us quick success in business or bring us more luck in love or make us more popular. Or we package it as painless medicine that will bring us miraculous healings or give us better health. I am not saying that faith has nothing to do with any of these matters. Faith affects attitudes, and attitudes have a tremendous influence in all of life. It is the nature of God to give, but when those benefits become the focus and the *reason* for our faith, we need to be confronted as Abraham was with the *claims* of faith. We need to ask ourselves, as Abraham asked himself, "How does my commitment to my faith compare with the commitment of others to their gods?" Perhaps we even need to ask ourselves how our commitment to God measures up to our own commitment to other interests. At what point are we willing to offer, to risk, as much for our faith as we are for other interests?

Part of what was involved in Abraham's impending sacrifice of Isaac was his willingness to place his own future in the hands of God. Isaac was his future. Abraham was an old man. Already he had been given a son when he was well past the years in which that was to be expected. The security of old age, the passing on of the heritage—all of this was wrapped up in Isaac. If Isaac were dead, all of that was gone. In his own time and culture, Abraham would have lived in vain.

Does this speak to our time? Not in the sense of trying to live our lives through our own children but in the sense of wanting to control our own future, to know what the next step of the path, the next bend of the trail will bring? What does it mean to surrender that which you thought contained your future? We who are so big on career planning and long-range goals and taking charge of our own lives have trouble with that!

Is this then a call for a placid folding of the hands and doing nothing? No, not at all. There is a place for planning and goal setting and all of that. We are not asked to go willy-nilly, hopscotching through life. *But there is a reminder here that there may also be a time for doing what God calls us to do in the present moment without requiring that the details of its impact on our future be submitted for our approval in advance.* Now does the story speak to our day? Now does it challenge us?

It is this response of Abraham that truly marks him as the "father of the faithful." Much has been made of his response of faith in the call that came early in his life—a call to leave family and kinships and familiar surroundings and to go forth, not knowing where, to follow in faith where God would lead him. To be sure, it took faith to do that. But with that first call came the promise, "I will make you a great nation, and I will bless you and make your name great, so that you will be a blessing." That was a call to adventure and risk, but it was also a call that held forth a promise. The call now was, in effect, to give back the promise—to obey without any reward save the knowledge of having obeyed.

I have a name for the kind of living that Abraham was

called upon to exemplify. I call it "living with open hands." I call it that because the open hand is one that does not grasp but is ready to yield up or to receive. It is the direct opposite of the "grab with gusto" philosophy that we hear so much about. Living with open hands means standing ready to do whatever is necessary in loyalty to God.

Abraham did not go through with the sacrifice of his son. That which he offered to God was returned to him. So it often is. In fact, the only things we really keep in this life are those things which we are willing to give to God. Other things may have us, but we have only that which we hold in the open hand, ready to use or ready to surrender back to God.

Life is a bit like the story I once heard about how they capture monkeys in a certain part of the world. They take a gourd with a narrow neck and hollow it out. Inside they place some food that monkeys like. The gourd is then fastened to a tree or to a stake in the ground. The monkey comes along and reaches into the gourd to grasp the goodies and discovers that it cannot get away. There is not a trap inside the gourd; it is just that the open hand will go in or out, but the closed or grasping one will not. The monkeys trap themselves because they will not let go. Grasp at life and you are trapped by what you will not let go of. True freedom is to be found in the open hand.

Harold DeWolfe tells the story of an administrator of a church related institution who says that the first requirement of a Christian administrator is that his resignation be always in his pocket. What does this mean? As soon as the position becomes indispensable to him, he is lost.

It is not a matter of being always ready to give up our lives in some twentieth-century, anti-Christian purge. Few of us will be faced with that. It is a matter of holding life in the open hand. Refrain from grasping it too tightly, and yet don't treat it cheaply as something to be cast away.

There is only one real way to do that, and that is the manner in which Abraham did it. Whether it be possessions, ambitions, dreams, hopes, or life itself, we must bring them to God as sacrifice, fully willing that they be received. It is then that we find, like Abraham, that what we give is often given back to us to enjoy more fully because we have given them away.

The supreme illustration came on a cross outside Jerusalem. Jesus had said in the upper room, "No man takes my life from me, I lay it down myself" (See John 10:18). And that which he gave to God in a manner that none other had ever given, was given back to him in a manner as was never done before.

"With Open Hands"—that is a free translation of what the Japanese call *karate*. When you have mastered that, they say, you can defend yourself against anyone. The Christian also has the secret of the open hand. It is the high art of self-surrender. When you have mastered that, you can defend yourself against any force in the world— even yourself.

*23*

# CHAPTER 2

# GOD SENT A WORM

Jonah 3 and 4

I sat on a rise of ground to the east of the city and waited for its destruction. This was going to be too good to miss. I glanced at the flourishing green vine that had grown up overnight to shade the little booth I had built for myself. I was thankful for the coolness it offered me as I sat waiting for judgment to come upon the city. Once or twice I debated moving back a little farther, in case the flames were too hot, but I decided that God would see to it that no harm came to me, a prophet. Besides, the shelter of the vine was too comfortable to leave.

Nineveh was beginning to stretch herself awake like some lazy animal in the morning sun. Housewives, their water jars on their shoulders, began to trickle out of doorways and down the streets to the village wells. Most of them had carried the water into the homes the night before. The few who had waited until now hardly paused along their way to gossip with their neighbors. The morning meal had to be prepared, but more important the sun would soon be blazing hot. It didn't take long here in this flat plain country along the Tigris Valley. The sun seemed to pop over the horizon one moment and into the middle of the sky the next.

Anyway, God shouldn't have much trouble getting this to burn. It certainly should be dried out enough!

I noticed a commotion at the well nearest me. A chariot had arrived, and the man in it was talking to the women. Some of the words drifted over to me, and I could piece together what he was saying. He was telling the women that Nineveh was to be destroyed, that its wickedness was so great that the God who ruled the world was going to purge the earth and send fire and brimstone upon the city. He told them that God had sent a prophet by the name of Jonah to tell them of their doom. I felt a bit pleased with myself, to hear my sermon of the past few days being quoted by an officer who was evidently high in the king's court.

I had been just a little frightened when I started preaching. One never knows what kind of reception one will get to a sermon topic as unpopular as the one I had to deliver. More than a few have been stoned or manhandled in some way or another. But the people looked so frightened that I soon got my courage back. It had almost been worth the journey to see the faces of the people filled with fear as I went from marketplace to marketplace.

The sermon got better as the days wore on. Before the

mission was over, I was able to paint a pretty realistic picture of just what they could expect.

What was that the man in the chariot just said? Something about "God repenting of anger"? I hadn't said that in my sermon. Someone was trying to mess up my work. I listened again. The charioteer began to read from a scroll. He raised his voice so all the people in the area could hear the words, and the words carried to where I was sitting, waiting for the destruction to begin.

> By the decree of the king and his nobles: Let neither man nor beast, herd nor flock, taste anything; let them not feed or drink water, but let man and beast be covered with sackcloth, and let them cry mightily to God; yea, let everyone turn from his evil way and from the violence which is in his hands . . . God may yet repent and turn from his fierce anger, so that we perish not.
>
> —Jonah 3:7-9

What kind of heresy was this? I hadn't said anything about God's changing his mind. That's the trouble with this preaching business. There is always someone around ready to misquote you. Of course, I knew that sometimes, after promising destruction, God had spared Israel, but they were the *special* people. This was a city of foreigners. Spare them, indeed! Ha! They would soon see what the God of Israel could do to those who were not the chosen ones.

A little later, I heard another disturbance in the streets,

as if some great procession were approaching. It came nearer, and I could hear that the mighty cry that was going up was not the usual jubilant shouts that accompanied a festival parade. There were wails, sounds of loud crying, pleas of ''Mercy'' and ''Forgive us.'' This was getting too good to be true—to see all these foreigners groveling in the dust, crying out for mercy before their doom, to see this mighty city broken and humbled when no armies camped on the plains outside the massive walls. I was glad now that I had not been permitted to escape to Tarshish in faraway Spain. I must have been out of my mind when I boarded that ship at Joppa.

The procession rounded a corner, and I could see it clearly. My, but that lead chariot was beautiful—all inlaid with gold and ivory and glistening in the sun! What was that on the side? By the beards of the prophets, it was the royal crest! The king himself was leading the procession. And he was dressed in sackcloth! A king in sackcloth. What a spectacle!

People were pouring out of houses, garbed in sackcloth and joining in the wailing. It looked as if half the city were involved. And the sun boiled down hotter than ever. So would God's wrath, I thought grimly.

Then it happened. In the midst of my thoughts about the uselessness of this display of tears and cries, I heard a voice. It was a voice I had come to know quite well in the past weeks. And God said, ''Because the people of Nineveh, from the least of them to the greatest of them, have

28

repented in dust and ashes and have turned from their evil ways, I will not do the thing towards them which I had intended to do.''

I could hardly believe my ears. It couldn't be true. Mercy for a bunch of foreigners! All this trip for nothing— the storm at sea, those three days and nights of terror and darkness, the long journey across the mountains, the days of preaching through the marketplaces—and now it all comes to this.

I slumped down where the shade of the vine was deepest. This was too much! I had half expected something like this might happen. That was why I started out for Tarshish instead of here in the first place. I knew God wouldn't really carry out his threat.

''You were relentless enough in getting me to come here when I didn't want to come! Where was your mercy then? Why don't you finish it off right and take my life? That would be a fitting end of it all—mercy for a bunch of foreign heathen and death for your faithful servant! Why don't you just kill me and be done with it?''

The sun was at its zenith now. The heat waves rose and danced across the sand, blurring my vision and the outline of the city, making it look like a reflection in a shimmering lake. I wiped the perspiration from my brow and looked at my vine. I had grown quite fond of it—so green and luxurious and sheltering. It was wonderful how it could grow here in the dust and heat, reminding one of coolness and courage and confidence. One needs reminders of these things in some of life's deserts. Maybe if I just have confidence and wait the city will be destroyed yet. Maybe....

What was this? The upper branches of the vines were turning brown! Before my very eyes, the plant was beginning to wither. The uppermost leaves and tendrils were already dead. I watched in horror as the sickness crept down the vine, shriveling, drying, dying as it came. What on earth could have caused it? Somehow my attention was drawn to a dark spot in the stem, a worm hole in the stem, just above the ground. Some little worm, no bigger than the tassel on my robe, was chewing its way through the center of the vine, destroying its life as it bored through the heartwood. I wanted to find that worm and crush it in my hands, to see its life ooze out before me as I saw the life of the plant slipping away.

Suddenly, I knew as surely as I sat there that God had sent that worm. This was no accidental pest that simply happened to find a choice morsel in its wandering path in search of food. Oh no! It fit too neatly into everything else that had happened. This was God's worm.

I had been like that plant. Back in Israel, I was comfortable and flourishing, content with my lot in life, giving little thought to anything outside the blessings that God had bestowed on Israel. I wasn't the richest man in my city, but I had everything I really needed. I had been...well, comfortable. That was a good word to describe it.

And God had sent a worm gnawing into my mind, urging me to go to Nineveh. Like the plant I had struggled in vain against its attack. Leave them alone, those Ninevites. Or send someone else, someone with less to lose or less to leave. Let one of their own priests speak to them. They have their own religion. Why mess them all up with another? Live and let live. They're nothing but a bunch of ignorant heathen anyway. For that matter, just go ahead and destroy them. Who cares? Why fool around with telling about it?

But no, the worm kept gnawing, chewing, eating away until in my mind I was withering like the plant. Poor plant, it couldn't even try to run away, like I did. Not that it would have done any good. Wherever it would have gone the worm would have gone, too. It had become a part of the plant, even as the worm God sent to gnaw at my mind became a part of me. I found that out when I tried to escape to Tarshish.

Suddenly I felt very sorry for the vine, and very angry at God. Why did God have to destroy such a beautiful thing? Here was a city full of heathen being spared and this beautiful plant withering and dying—dying the kind of death I came expecting to see visited on the Ninevites. Why couldn't God have spared the plant? Let the heathen Ninevites perish. Why did God have to bother me? I could have stayed at ease in Israel. Must the blest of the earth always bear the burdens of the less fortunate?

I heard the voice again. It came to me in tones like I had never heard before. The voice was like some kind father explaining something to a small child, explaining some lesson the child had failed again to learn:

> Jonah, you pity the plant. You did not labor for it; you did not create it. It came into being overnight and perished in a night. Should I not have pity on Nineveh, that great city in which there are more than 120,000 persons who do not even know their right hand from their left? They may be different from you, Jonah, but they are part of my creation.
> —Jonah 3:10-11, AP

For a moment I could not move. The voice, the infinite patience, the wonderful truth I suddenly saw was too much. Then I bowed my head. With tears flowing down my face I prayed, "O Lord, I did not know you loved them, too. Amen."

# CHAPTER 3

# THE INNKEEPER'S PRAYER

## Luke 2:7

Matthias, the innkeeper, was traveling home from Jerusalem, but his thoughts were on Bethlehem. He was walking in the springtime, but he was thinking of a winter evening long ago. He had just witnessed a cross on a hillside, but his thoughts were of a manger in a stable behind his inn. He had just seen three men die, but he was remembering the night when one of them was born. Some had said that Calvary was the end, but Matthias was thinking of a beginning.

He noticed a young boy herding a flock of sheep across the road ahead of him, bound for some higher pasture, now that the grass was growing again. The young lambs scampered in the sunlight. It was this scene that had triggered his thoughts back across the years. It had been the bleating of a lamb that had awakened him that night so long ago.

## WRITINGS IN THE DUST

He could remember the scene as if it were yesterday. The day had been about as trying a day as he cared to go through. The Roman Emperor, sitting in his ivory palace in Rome, dreaming up things to keep his governors and officers busy and give them less time to think about the wretchedness of some of their assignments, had come up with the idea of taking a census of the empire. To complicate matters, people had to return to the city of their birth to register. Of course, that made for good business for innkeepers, but Matthias would have preferred his business spread out a little.

As if fighting all day to get a little more work out of his servants (who he declared were born tired) had not been enough, there had been the arguments with the rich travelers who somehow always managed to arrive late and expect the finest accommodations. They seemed confident that their money would take care of them! No, that wasn't really fair. There had only been one who had made such a fuss about it, lording over everyone his influence with the governor until Matthias had finally given him his own room and moved into a storage shed himself in order to have peace in the house.

After such a day he had been irritable when he went to bed. His head seemed to have scarcely touched the mat when he heard the click of hooves on the stone in the courtyard and a few minutes later a tapping on the doorpost. He tried to ignore it, but the tapping came again. With a groan he roused himself and wrapped his cloak about him.

**34**

## THE INNKEEPER'S PRAYER

It shouldn't take long to get rid of them, he thought. There was simply nothing left.

He had opened the door and growled, "All the rooms are taken." He was immediately sorry he had spoken so gruffly. The man leading the little donkey was apologizing for disturbing them so late at night. He pointed to the woman on the donkey and explained that they had hurried as fast as they could, but her condition would not permit a rapid pace. Even so, he was afraid that the jolting had been too much for her. They were expecting a child any day now. Given a choice, they would never have traveled at such a time as this. But the decree had said, "every man to his own city," and he was of the house of David. Wasn't there something he could offer them?

No, nothing. He was sorry, but even his own room was occupied. There was nothing at all. The man—he had said his name was Joseph—had nodded and turned to go. Matthias was never sure just what it was that prompted him to call after them. Perhaps it was the disappointment so evident in the man's face as he turned to his wife. Maybe it was the way she smiled at him to let him know that she understood. It may have been simply that he was tired of arguing, and here were two who believed him when he said he had no room. At any rate, the words were out before he knew it: "There's a stable in the back. It isn't very much, but you are welcome to such as it is."

You would have thought he had offered them his own room, they were so grateful. They had thanked him so profusely that he had told them to help themselves to fresh straw and a lamp. After he had lain down again, he wondered if he had made a mistake in that. They might upset the thing and burn the place down. But he was too tired to get up and go out and ask for it back. He had fallen asleep before he could debate the matter very long.

It must have been four or five hours later that he had heard the noise in the courtyard that awakened him. He had sat there in the darkness for a moment, thinking at first that it had been a dream. Then he heard it again—the bleating of a lamb. He was wide awake now. Quickly he had hurried to the window, ready to call the alarm in case it were robbers grown more bold and seeking to rob the inn. He nearly fell out the window when he saw the group of shepherds standing around the entrance to the stable. Their garments told him their trade and two of them carried the long crooked hooks they used for walking and guiding the flock. It was not the season for lambs, but evidently one had come out of due time and could not be left alone. One of the shepherds carried it on his shoulder.

Throwing on his robe, Matthias hurried out into the courtyard and around to the stable. As he turned the corner of the house, he stopped. The shepherds were kneeling in the entrance to the cattle stall. Filled with amazement, he walked slowly forward and peered inside. The man, Joseph, was talking with one of the shepherds. He could still remember the words of the shepherd.

"We were afraid," the man had said as Matthias walked

inside. "And the angel said to us, 'Do not be afraid! Listen, I bring you glorious news of great joy, which is for all people. This very day, in David's city, a savior has been born for you. He is Christ, the Lord. Let this prove it to you; you will find a baby, wrapped up and lying in a manger.' "

"And suddenly, there appeared with the angel a vast host of the armies of heaven, praising God, saying, 'Glory to God in the highest Heaven! Peace on earth among men of good will'."

"And so we left our flocks and came straight to Bethlehem to see this thing which the Lord had made known to us."

It was then that Matthias glimpsed the baby. He was so enfolded in his mother's cloak that he had hardly seen him at first. He tried now to recall if there had been anything special about him, but he couldn't remember. He looked like all the newly-born children he had seen—pink and helpless and sleeping. He did remember how he had started when Joseph had said quietly to the shepherds, "We were told to call his name Jesus, for he shall save his people from their sins."

Matthias was glad that he had brought them into the house the next day, as soon as the first traveler had departed and a room was empty. There he had talked much with Joseph and Mary about the child who had been born in his manger, and it was in his house a few days later that he beheld the second wonder. Men from the East had come to the house and brought their gifts and worshiped the child. They also brought the disturbing news of Herod's concern with the child. A few days later Joseph announced that he had been warned in a dream to take the child and flee to Egypt. Matthias could still hear the cries of the mothers when Herod's soldiers came.

The years had passed, and Matthias had not seen Joseph or Mary again. Other visitors came to his inn in Bethlehem. Many listened to his story of the wonderful birth. Then, one day, when he was rapidly becoming an old man, he heard of a prophet who had come out of Nazareth, a prophet by the name of Jesus. Of course, it could have been only a coincidence, because there were many prophets in those days. The name *Jesus* was not uncommon. But Matthias had made inquiries and he was sure that it was the same one.

Matthias joined the crowds going out to listen to Jesus. The innkeeper had heard him preach only one sermon, but he would never forget what Jesus had said in it. It made him think again of a traveler and his wife asking for a room in an inn. He had been talking about people being rewarded for the things they had done to him, even though they claimed they had never seen him. He had said, "Inasmuch as ye have done it unto one of the least of these my brethren, ye have done it unto me" (Matt. 25:40). How true it was! The Christ had come to see him, and he had almost never known it. If it hadn't been for the bleating of a lamb, he would have missed it.

**38**

## THE INNKEEPER'S PRAYER

The journey had passed much faster than he thought. Here he was at the entrance to his inn. His mind and heart still full of many things, he walked around the house to the little stable in the rear. He often went there to think. It seemed a peaceful place. Now he thought again of what he had seen in Jerusalem. It was hard to believe that the tiny life he had seen nestled here in the hay had ended so tragically. He had heard some of the followers talking afterwards and some of them seemed to think that it was all over now.

Matthias wasn't sure. He had heard the exchange of a few words between Jesus and one of the thieves crucified with him. The man had looked at him and whispered, "Lord, remember me when you come into your kingdom."

Jesus had answered, "Truly, I say to you, you will be with me today in paradise." There seemed to be a certainty about him that even his death could not completely take away. What if he were right and his enemies were wrong, Matthias thought. To think that it started in a manger!

Matthias dropped to his knees near the spot where Mary and the child had lain so long ago. He began to pray, "O Lord, I am sorry that my inn was full when you came into the world. I didn't know that it was you, seeking entrance, or I would have found room for you somehow. I would have cast out someone else and made room for you. But you were so unassuming that I thought it was simply another traveler making another demand on my time. I

*39*

considered you of no more importance than all the others. My world was such a busy place, and all the tasks seemed so important.

"But I am wiser now than then. I have learned that things are often not what they seem, and what seems important may be nothing compared to that which really matters."

He paused in his prayer, and then continued.

"O Lord, forgive the sins of one who offered you only a manger for your birth but now offers you the fullness of his heart."

# CHAPTER 4

# MIDDLE MAN

John 1:35-42; 6:8-9; 12:9-22

You know my brother better than you know me. My name is Andrew, brother of Simon Peter, the one whom Jesus called "the Rock." Like Simon, I was a fisherman until that day that the Master came and told us to follow him. Not that that was the first time we had met him, mind you. Not even Simon was so impetuous as that!

We had heard him when he taught by the lake, and we had talked about what he said among ourselves. We had not really thought all that much of leaving everything to go after him. That was very much a decision made the day he called. There was something in his look, in his voice—I can't really explain it, but it was there and it spoke to something deep within *me*.

I'm not sure what he saw in me to be one of the twelve. That was a rather special group of men, and I didn't have the leadership ability of my brother or the deep devotional and spiritual qualities of John or the skill of managing money or the training that some of the others had.

As is often the case of those surrounded by people of outstanding skills, I considered myself rather plain. One gift I had. People found me easy to talk to. People—people like me, who would never have the courage to go barging up to Jesus himself—would come to me, as if they had known me all their lives.

There was that day on the hillsides around the Sea of Galilee. It was during the days when the Master's popularity was at its height and people flocked after him until he could have no time to rest or renew himself except by withdrawing into some remote place to escape. He tried to escape this time by going to the other side of the sea but to no avail. The multitudes were there as well, calling out to be healed, wanting to hear him teach. He took a few of us up into the hills a bit farther, but they came there, too!

Jesus was talking with Philip about how we could feed so many people, as if their foolishness in coming so far without food was our fault. Philip replied that it would take more money than we had to give everyone a little, much less really feed them. I felt a tug at my sleeve and found a young lad standing there holding a basket in which he had five barley loaves and two fish. He had no doubt followed the crowd to try to sell his wares, but after hearing Jesus talk he was moved to offer what he had.

Five barley loaves and two fish! If it had been just our little group of disciples it might have been enough. In this multitude it was laughable, but I didn't laugh. Something in the boy's eyes told me that this was serious business to him, so I took him to Jesus.

I don't really know what I expected the Master to do about it. I said as much. But the lad clearly expected me to do something, and I thought the Master should know about such generosity. Mind you, I didn't claim credit for the miracle that followed, but I did take the boy to Jesus.

Then there was the day in Jerusalem when the Greeks came. Passover feast was just a few days away, and Jesus' entry into Jerusalem was a spectacle I shall remember as long as I live. We came down the slopes of Gethsemane and across the Kidron Valley toward the gate nearest the temple. The people poured out of the city to meet us, strewing the road with branches of the palm trees along the way and shouting, "Hosanna! Blessed be he who comes in the name of the Lord, even the King of Israel." It was a glorious day!

Lazarus was there, and that added to the fervor of the crowd since Jesus had raised him from the dead only a few days before and word had spread like wildfire. The Pharisees would like to have ended it all right there, but they were afraid of the wrath of the people. I heard one of them say as much to some others: "You see that? You can do nothing; look, the world has gone after him" (John. 12:19, AP).

As if to give evidence to the claim, Philip called to me and introduced me to some Greeks who had come to worship at the feast and heard about Jesus. They wanted to meet him. I suppose they went to Philip because he was a bit Greek himself, and I don't know why Philip came to me instead of taking them to Jesus himself, but he did. So I took them to Jesus.

But the introduction I remember most was one that preceded all of these. It was I who introduced Simon to Jesus. I had heard of Jesus first from John the Baptizer. I had been his disciple before I became a disciple of Jesus, and one day as a friend and I were with John he pointed to another man who was passing by and called him, ''The Lamb of God.'' We left John then and followed the stranger. He invited us to the place where he was staying that night and we spent the evening listening to his teaching. When we left the next day I knew this was something I could not keep to myself. Simon and I had talked many times of the One who was to come, and I was convinced that this Jesus was that person. I said as much to Simon: ''We have found the Messiah!''

And then, practically dragging him after me in my haste to share what I had found, I brought my brother to the Master.

It isn't always easy to convince those in your own household, but Simon and I had always been rather close. I was willing to be overshadowed by him a bit, content with a little less attention than Simon seemed to need. I remember how Jesus made the word play on his name, Peter, which means ''rock'' in Greek and Cephas, which means the same thing in Aramaic. I didn't know all that

## MIDDLE MAN

Jesus' words about my brother portended that day, but I have always been proud that I was the one who brought him to meet the Master.

My ability doesn't match that of others when it comes to leadership or preaching to the masses or organizing to spread the word into some new land. But I can relate to people in ways that are open and nonthreatening to them. People with needs of heart and soul may seek me out, and I can introduce them to the Master in some quiet way.

And who knows? Perhaps some of those I bring to our Lord will accomplish greater things for him that I could ever do. What does it matter who gets the credit? Does it matter even if it is known that I brought them together? I do not care so much that they remember me—only that they know him.

# CHAPTER 5

# A MAN UP A TREE

Luke 19:1-10

Zacchaeus hurried through the streets of Jericho like a man obsessed. His short legs made his effort seem even more intensive than it was, and some small boys pointed and laughed and briefly imitated his hurried gait. He would have liked to stop to scold them, but it was only a passing thought. He had no time. Something far more important filled his mind. He had to get where he could see this Galilean up close.

For days his mind had been filled with thoughts that would not let him rest. He had heard the teacher from the fringes of the crowd—now he wanted to see him close at hand. "From the fringes, there's where I've always been," he thought bitterly. His small stature always seemed to keep him there. He lived in a world of backs and shoulders and elbows! Others always got there first, and he could never see what he came to see as the backs of others always blocked his view.

It had been that way again today. He had inquired

around after he had heard this man before and had learned
when he was coming to Jericho. He even found out where
he would be coming from so he would know where he
might wait to see him, but he was too late again. This
teacher from Nazareth was too popular or at least too
much of a curiosity. In that incredible word-of-mouth
phenomenon that defied the laws of logic, word seemed to
flow ahead of him like sandpipers before the tide. No
matter where he went or when, the crowds were there to
press upon him or touch him or to demand some new
miracle. By the time Zacchaeus had reached the place he
thought he could see the man, the crowds were already there,
three deep in most places. Not that the second and third
layer mattered much, Zacchaeus had his problems when
they were one deep. Others could look over shoulders or
between heads. He always found himself staring at backs.

It had been that way all of his life, a sort of perpetual
childhood as far as accessibility was concerned. He could
never seem to walk as fast or reach as far or give the
appearance of strength and confidence that a world built on
power and might seemed to think was important. He
couldn't even look people in the eye. He could tell you a
lot about double chins and flaring nostrils, but that never
seemed to compensate.

He had compensated, however. He had found ways to
make up for what he felt was his inadequacy. He found a
position of power and used it in such a way that people had
to look up to him figuratively, if not literally. He became a

tax collector. Oh, the position had cost him money, but people seemed willing to accept a small man's money quickly enough. A few coins here and a few more there, and the job was his. The position gave him what he wanted. The fact that it paid well besides was somewhat incidental, although he soon found that wealth gave him power beyond his stature too.

The money came because he could name the taxes that people had to pay. Rome told him how much *they* wanted, and his own income was dependent upon how much additional he could collect. But the power of Rome was behind that collection. As long as he wasn't *too* greedy, no one would complain because they did not want trouble with Rome. After all, people didn't know what their real taxes were anyway. Their taxes were whatever he said they were. That was his power. While he liked the income, it was the power that stirred him most. People hated him for his power and his wealth and the common knowledge that corruption was part of the office. But Zacchaeus had long ago decided that he would rather be hated for being powerful and rich than be despised for appearing small and weak.

Then he had heard this Jesus, and he had not rested since. He did not normally make many public appearances. Between his office in life and his physical problem, such events were mostly unpleasant. Nobody liked a tax collector, and everyone seemed to belittle small people. So he usually stayed at home—except when he went out to collect the taxes, of course. He walked taller then. While they could hate him, it would be after they had paid him! But when he heard that one of this teacher's followers was a tax collector, he could not stay away. ''Who was this who could accept a tax collector?'' he remembered thinking. It had been so long since he had had an invitation to someone's house that he could hardly remember what other houses looked like. No one ever came to dine with him. They treated him as if he had leprosy. But this teacher—it was even said that he had refused to condemn a woman taken in adultery. Zacchaeus wasn't sure what he thought about that, but anyone who would let a tax collector travel with him couldn't be all bad! He certainly had wanted to see for himself.

The first time had been a frustration—too many people for him to get close enough to see. But he had heard. And what he heard brought a host of questions and uncertainties flooding in upon him. Now he wanted to see him. He wanted to see with his own eyes, close up, this man whose words had put his life to question and moved him deeply. He wanted to look into his eyes and hear him speak again. Then he would know. It was one thing to hear words and admonitions from a distance—the impersonal advice of some remote orator who might be living in luxury while he advocated sacrifice. It was another matter to watch that life and test it against its own precepts. Somehow Zacchaeus knew that if he could just get close enough to look into his eyes, he would know. So he had checked and planned and tried to beat the crowds, but he had failed. His efforts to squeeze through between the people already there were futile.

He had turned away in disappointment and started to go home when he remembered the sycamore tree. It grew along the road down which the procession was moving. He had played in it as a boy, enjoying the added height it gave him, and he recalled that the branches were close enough to the ground that he could struggle and pull his way up into it. He thought he could beat the crowd there because the teacher's very presence slowed their movement. No one wanted to leave the teacher to get in front, and the crowd was piling up behind him now. People were moving down the street to get a little closer. The tree was far enough ahead that Zaccheaus thought he could get to it before the crowds, and he had hurried on.

He saw the tree ahead of him, just as he remembered it—its friendly branches reaching out to him and near enough to the road that he should have no trouble seeing. He paused a moment to catch his breath but not for long. He didn't want to be pushed aside again.

He was in the tree now, above the heads of even the tallest of the crowd. He liked that. He could remember the pleasant feeling that it had given him as a child—looking down for a change, instead of always craning his neck to look up. That was the feeling that his money and his power and his authority gave him now. The sycamore was the tree of his childhood, but he had found taller trees in

**51**

the following years. As a youth, he had climbed higher and higher with each passing year.

He felt some beads of sweat on his brow, and decided he was high enough. Pushing up from some forgotten corner of his mind, there came the memory of the time he had climbed so high in this tree that he despaired of ever getting down. He had stretched and pulled and fallen only to nearly kill himself coming down. Sometimes trees are easier to get into than to get out of. He hadn't thought of that day in years, and he wondered why it came to mind now. Just being in the tree again, he supposed. The voices of the crowd called him back to the moment.

The crowd was almost even with him now, surging around the tree, trying to keep close enough to see or touch the teacher, stumbling and pushing one another aside. He was going to pass right beneath him! He had been afraid that he might be all the way on the other side of the road, but he was headed right for the tree. Zacchaeus was concentrating on the features of the teacher when suddenly a shock went through him. Eyes were looking at him. It was not just a glance around like one might do at bystanders and people along the way. It was a focusing of attention that blotted out everything else and made it seem as if the two of them were the only people in the world.

There was no disgust or ridicule or dislike in the look. They were friendly eyes that looked into his. Eyes that seemed to crack open the hardened surface of his life like the shell of a nut and lay bare his soul. It was not just that this man seemed to see inside of him; it was as if Zacchaeus were looking inside of himself through Jesus' eyes. He didn't like what he saw.

He had always seen himself as a little man struggling to survive in a big peoples' world, being stepped on and pushed aside and passed by. Suddenly he saw that he was one who pushed and stepped on and passed by others through the power and position he had achieved. Many of those he taxed the hardest were the people who would argue with him least. He never went beyond their ability, but he knew their limits awfully well. He knew that many had to deny their families in order to meet his demands. The rich might have enough influence of their own to get back at him, so he walked more carefully there. But the poor had little choice, so that was where he put the pressure.

In his efforts to compensate for his smallness he had become what he hated—a pusher and crusher of those smaller than himself. Zacchaeus was sickened by what he saw. Why do we so often become what we hate in some disguised form? Or is the reason we hate some things to be found in the transferal or magnification of our faults into the lives of others? Are our strongest hates our secret sins?

A voice cut through his preoccupation with his guilt. "Zacchaeus! Make haste and come down. I need to stay at your house today." Zacchaeus nearly fell out of the tree.

To have dinner with the teacher? It was unbelievable! And not at his own invitation, but at Jesus'. Was he mocking him! No, this man would not stoop to mocking.

He heard one of the crowd mutter the very thought that had been in his own mind, "He is going to eat in the house of a man who is a sinner!" And that, he suddenly realized, was the whole point about this man. He did not look up or down at people. He looked into people. He saw their hearts, their sins, but he also saw their hopes and their dreams and their longings.

Zacchaeus looked again into those eyes that mirrored his soul. This time he saw something else. This time he saw the Zacchaeus that still could be—a man whose size would be measured not in feet and inches or breadth of shoulder or might of arm, but in integrity and spirit and compassion. In fact, Zacchaeus did not think in sizes of any kind in that moment. It did not matter that he was smaller than other men; it would not matter if he were larger than other men. He no longer needed to be richer or more powerful or more feared. It was enough that this man called him friend.

And so Zacchaeus came down from the tree. He no longer needed the sycamore. He no longer needed his wealth and his power and his authority. He no longer needed any of his trees. He was as tall as any man needed to be. He could reach the kingdom of God.

# CHAPTER 6

# A GUEST IN MY OWN HOUSE

### Luke 10:38-42

I am Mary of Bethany.

It was my brother Lazarus whom Jesus raised from the dead. Our home in Bethany was one of Jesus' favorite stopping places. Being near to Jerusalem, it provided a place of rest and perhaps escape from the pressures of the crowds and the harassment of his enemies. He could relax and renew his energy a bit. He sometimes said that he had no place to lay his head, but that didn't mean that he wasn't always welcome in our home. We felt honored to have him come.

Some have thought that I was lazy. Why? I chose to sit at Jesus' feet when he came to visit with us, instead of helping my sister Martha prepare the meal to serve him. I can be criticized for that, I suppose, but actually, Jesus never came for fancy meals. I had learned that. Martha hadn't. She still thought of him as a guest in our house. I had come to recognize that it is we who are really the guests, and he who is the host. It is he who feeds us—not in meat and bread, but in words and in understanding. He once said, "I have meat to eat that you do not know about." That was what he fed to me when I was receptive to it.

Mind you, that didn't mean a life of doing nothing but sitting and listening! But after I listened for awhile, I saw much more clearly what needed doing! Many times—until I learned better—I would rush off in busyness and discover later that I had missed what needed doing most. Besides, I had a strange feeling that he wasn't going to be available much longer.

Even now, I find it helpful to set aside a regular time for prayer and meditation. When the press of some decision comes and I don't have much time to think, I have conditioned myself and prepared myself in such a way that I can do the right thing automatically. Not that I don't make the wrong choice sometimes. But I make fewer bad choices than I would if I didn't use time to communicate with my Lord.

I don't make light of Martha and her labor. She loves him, too. But as Jesus told her, it is easy to be distracted by much serving, to become anxious and troubled by things that are not really all that important. People need food to live, but if they have no purpose for living, no understanding beyond survival, what good is it to give them food?

## A GUEST IN MY OWN HOUSE

I remember one time when Jesus watched a great crowd of people turn and go away angry and disappointed because he had no food to give them. He turned to the disciples and a few of us who were with him and said with disappointment evident in his voice, "Will you also go away?"

One of the twelve—I think it was Peter—answered him, "Lord, to whom can we go? You have the words of life." That is my feeling, too. We don't need to feed him, he has food for us. You there, in your busyness, have you taken time lately to sit at his feet and learn of him? That is where discipleship begins. The service will come soon enough.

I am one of the women who walked with Jesus—women whose lives were touched and changed on his journey from Bethlehem to Calvary. I invite others to open their lives to the Christ who forgives us and cleanses us and invites us to sit at his feet and learn of him.

Still, across the centuries, he comes to us—this guest who is the host.

CHAPTER 7

# ON WAKING UP IN A PIGSTY

### Luke 15:11-24

It was the smell that finally did it.

Not that he hadn't known where he was. You can't live with pigs and feed pigs and water pigs and hear their grunting and snorting, watch the shoving and crowding about the troughs, and listen to the strange snuffling, slurping sounds they make as they eat, without realizing that you are in a pigsty. But sometimes there is a difference between knowledge and real awareness. He had always known—today he recognized the fact for what it was. He was living in a pigsty. He had been there for several weeks now—ever since his money had run out and his so-called friends had left him to find someone who still had a few coins with which to entertain them. He had tried asking them for help, but they had laughed at him and pushed him aside.

It was hard to believe that he had been actually starving

**59**

when this Gentile merchant had offered him a job feeding pigs. Hunger will drive a man awfully far.

A Jew feeding pigs! And not only feeding them but practically at the point of eating their food—he was that hungry. The carob pods were really all that had kept him alive, and he guessed they were clean enough when he picked them out of the shellings before he carried them to the pigpens. There were even a few beans here and there in some of them. The truth of the matter was, if he hadn't been able to have his pick ahead of time, he would have been willing to get down on all fours and eat with pigs. He had been almost to that point when he first came to work. He was that hungry.

But today the smell finally got to him. It was not that he had just become aware of it. No. The odor had hit him like a physical blow in the face the first day he came, but then he was too bad off to care. He knew what his religion felt about pigs. But when you have no hope and you are literally starving to death, some of the finer points of religion slip by—especially when religion hasn't been all that important to you anyway. If you hadn't paid much attention to the commandments themselves, associating with pigs didn't seem too devastating. Besides, when you come right down to it, he hadn't *eaten* pig—just eaten *with* them.

He guessed he must be getting stronger if he could bother to worry about it. He had heard that only people who have some cause for hope bother to make a fuss about their condition. The rich sometimes think that the poor are content when they are really only too depressed to hope. Those who sometimes seem to lash out after they have been helped and so frustrate their benefactors are often only expressing the anger and frustration that they had been too emotionally drained to express before. He had always had a hard time understanding that—until now.

It had been the same way with the pig smell. It had been bad enough all along that neighbors a half-mile down wind complained. But he hadn't said a thing. He had learned to do what he had to do to survive and stay up wind as much as possible, but he hadn't rebelled against it. Not until today. Today he suddenly decided that he couldn't stand pigs any longer. He remembered some of the things he had been taught as a boy. The Lord God had forbidden his people to eat pork. In Leviticus, it was clearly written:

> The swine, because it parts the hoof and is cloven-footed but does not chew the cud, is unclean to you. Of their flesh you shall not eat, and their carcasses you shall not touch; they are unclean to you.
>
> —Leviticus 11:7-8

For some reason, the story of the seven brothers came to his mind. It had been in the time of Judas Maccabaeus, when the Syrians had oppressed his people. Circumcision had been forbidden, and the eating of pork was forced upon the leading families. One women with seven sons was commanded to eat pork and refused. One by one they

**61**

were horribly mutilated and finally killed, with the death of each being used as added pressure for the survivors to eat the pork. All seven plus the mother went to their deaths rather than eat the forbidden food. His teachers and his father had told the gruesome story many times to illustrate the courage of his people and the importance of the law. Some could even have escaped death by pretending to eat and refused to do so.

All that over a bite of pork! It was incredible. He looked up at the mud brick wall beside him. He was in one of the currently unused shelters that sometimes housed a sow with piglets to keep the others from trampling them or an old boar from eating them. Fortunately, it was on the upwind side of the farm. A passing thought—did even young pigs have to get used to the smell of pigpens? He had said something about it to the merchant, but he had only glared and said that it smelled like money to him!

His gaze was drawn to some scratches in the surface of the brick. With a bit of a start, he recognized it as his own name. He hadn't remembered scratching it there, but obviously he had. Probably on one of those early days. He wondered how many and what kind of other places carried his name? What was it that made a man write his name in nameless places, leaving little pieces of himself scattered across the world? Why write his name? Didn't he know who he was? A man could write his name in a thousand places and still not know who or where he was. Identity wasn't something that you carried in your pocket or on a chain around your neck or that you established by carving your name on pigpens or brothel walls, or for that matter on pyramids or palaces. Identity came from inside. All other fuss and bother were like scratches on the wall of a pigsty. If you didn't know who you were from the inside, you'd never find it by looking for scratches, he thought. Some other pig would come along and rub against it a few times, and it would be gone.

Some *other* pig? What had made him think of it that way? He wasn't an animal! Or was he? How had the condition in which he had arrived been different from the animals he was taking care of? They only thought about their own appetites: pushing, crowding, grunting, wallowing in mud, squealing, eating. He had even seen them devour one another when one was knocked down in the struggle and somehow injured. There seemed to be some lurking evil that pounced on any weakness and devoured it.

Perhaps the pushing was all too much like what he had been through in the past months. "Give me my inheritance," he had demanded of his father. What but swinish appetite had caused him to do that? His father wasn't dead—not even sick. The "inheritance" wasn't his until his father had no more use for it. And even then, it wasn't his unless his father chose to bestow it. Knowing the kind of man his father was, he would give it to him. But he had presumed on that good man's kindly soul as much as the pigs seemed to assume that the carob pods grew just for their consumption. And he had soon learned that those he had fallen in with cared little more for him than one pig seemed to care for another.

A loud squealing in the outside pens brought him quickly to his feet, and he dashed outside to break up a fight before one of the pigs was killed or badly injured. A few kicks and blows with the long club he kept handy and the fighters were distracted enough to go about other things, one going back to eating again and the other to rub on a post.

He didn't go back into the shelter. The sun was high in the sky, and the road beckoned him someplace else—someplace away from pigs.

He thought again of the story of the seven brothers and what they had endured rather than eat pork. Then, for some reason, the thought came to him that it wasn't really over eating pork at all. It was over keeping the law of God. The law simply happened to be "don't eat pork." But the issue wasn't pork—it was obedience. Why had he never realized that before? Why had he always complained and picked at the details of the rules instead of realizing that the real issue was an obedient spirit? The difficulty was not in refraining from eating pork so much as it was *wanting* to refrain from eating pork or from committing adultery or from lying or from violating the Sabbath, or any of the rest of the commandments. The issue was rooted in the will more than in the actions. It was almost as though when one came to terms with that attitude, the weight of the law itself was lifted.

## ON WAKING UP IN A PIGSTY

Why had he rebelled so against his father? The tasks his father gave him were not difficult—certainly much less burdensome than tending swine! And his food was certainly more than carob pods! Even his father's servants got better than that! It was not the deeds he was told to do that caused him to rebel. It was the fact that he was told to do them. He had wanted to rule his own life absolutely, and he had learned that it was not so simple as that. He had learned that appetite and impulse were sterner masters than the rules he had thrown over for them.

He would go back to his father's house. He would go home. The word brought a lump to his throat, and he brushed impatiently at a bit of dust that seemed to have gotten into his eyes, making them water.

He had no claim there, he knew. He had forfeited that, demanding his due, leaving his brother to do the work, his father to worry in old age. Perhaps he could work there as a hired servant. It would be a better job than feeding pigs! And he would be home, even if he was a servant instead of a son.

There seemed to be dust in his eyes again as he started down the road, and he didn't notice the strange contradiction between the first word of the speech that he was rehearsing and all the words that followed:

"Father, I have sinned against heaven and in your sight."

"I am no longer worthy to be called your son; make me as one of your hired servants."

A few days later, the pigsty far behind him, he spoke

the speech to the familiar figure that came running down the road to meet him. But the one who embraced him heard his opening word: "Father. . . ."

And the awakening that had begun in the pigsty was completed.

# CHAPTER 8

# WISDOM AT A WELL

## John 4:1-26

You will find my case history in the Gospel of John. The writer does not give me a name. I am simply called "a woman of Samaria." That, in itself, is symbolic. People such as I, who were considered outcasts and inferior in Jesus' day, were not regarded as individuals. We were not persons in our own right but simply one of a group of "them."

Samaritans and Jews are not the only examples. Roman and barbarian, black and white, rich and poor, educated and uneducated. It is always easier to ridicule and criticize the "other side" if you first divest them of personality, or give them all the same personality, which accomplishes the same thing. Haven't you noticed in war that the enemy is never an *individual* but always "they"?

Jesus never acted that way. He made me a person. I couldn't understand it at first. He was obviously Jewish, and Jews had had no dealings with Samaritans for centuries. I reminded him of that, but he wouldn't be drawn into that old controversy between the races. He wouldn't permit me to hide behind my race any more than he would follow the too-familiar pattern of prejudice that I had come to expect from his race. Treating me as an individual meant that I had to confront my own failings and not pass them off as the result of the way others treated me. You see, he not only saw me as a person, he made me see myself.

His disciples were surprised to find him talking to me when they returned. And while they didn't say anything, I could tell that they disapproved. Because I was a woman, probably. That is another "they" category that caused a lot of pain and covered a great deal of wrong.

I confess that I was surprised to sense that attitude in them since they were his followers. I thought they would be a bit more like him, but I guess that followers don't always measure up to their leader, at least not at first. They sometimes continue to operate out of old prejudices and habits and try to fit people into molds and stereotypes. But there, you see, I'm doing the same thing. I'm saying "they" instead of looking at them individually!

I keep trying to remind myself that even when they don't measure up I am called to love those who act in unworthy ways, just as they are called to love me; but it is difficult to do. To dislike people for the way they act or what they do, that's understandable, at least. But to dislike them because of their race or color or their situation in life or the group they belong to—how can they do anything about that? Who can choose how and when and in what circumstances they are born? Maybe that is why this teacher seems to show a bias toward the outcasts—they are so often rejected for reasons over which they have no control. The lepers, the poor, the physically impaired, in short, the disenfranchised—they seemed to have a special claim on Jesus.

I've had another thought. Maybe it's just that our status in society helps us avoid too much pride. Maybe we see our need for God better than those who have all the praise and power of the world. At any rate, he treated me like a person. And the fact that I was a Samaritan and a woman was no hindrance to God's love.

Jesus asked me for a cup of water at the well that day, and I gave him one. He said that whoever drank of the water that I gave would be thirsty again, so I suppose he has asked others for cups of water since that day and used his request to talk to them as he did to me. But I asked him for eternal water, too, and my thirst was quenched, just as he said it would be.

# CHAPTER 9

# WRITINGS IN THE DUST

### John 8:3-11

The streets of Jerusalem were always dusty. The daily traffic of tens of thousands of human sandals, plus the sharper hooves of sheep and goats, to say nothing of the heavier plodding of the camels and donkeys, ground the hard-packed earth into powder. On the holy days only the press of the multitudes kept the dust from filling nose and ears and eyes. Even so, it coated clothing and body inescapably. Only the infrequent rains brought relief, and that was only for the briefest season. People became used to the dust, however. People become used to almost anything, given time enough and circumstance enough.

The man who stood in the middle of the street was used to dust. He had known it all his life—the dust of the earthen yards in which he played as a child, the rock dust of the roads from Bethany to Jerusalem or Bethlehem or the surrounding towns, the dust of wood from his father's carpenter shop in Nazareth. He had walked in dust and lived in dust for more than thirty years now. He stood in dust and looked at the woman before him.

## WRITINGS IN THE DUST

The woman knew dust, too—not only the dust of the streets and towns as he knew them but the dry dust of despair that came from being a woman in her day with no husband or family in her life. She knew the tasteless dust of hunger, and she knew that clinging dust of sin that came from the way she now made her meager living. She stood where her accusers had pushed her, in the dust at the feet of the teacher whom they hated because of his popularity with the people. She knew that they hated him because of what she had heard them say as they brought her here. She sensed somehow that they did not really care very much about the fact that they had caught her in the act of adultery. Their hatred of this man far overshadowed any revulsion at her sin. They only wanted to get at this teacher. "If he condemns her," she had heard them say, "we can report him to Rome as one who sets himself up as a judge. If he frees her, he will show himself to the people as one who disregards the law of Moses."

From something one of them had said, she even wondered if they had paid the man with whom they had found her and promised him immunity in return for betraying her. A flash of anger went through her. She wondered where her husband was. She was a married woman, or she would not be in this predicament. Her husband had been gone these many months now, and she had not known where he was any of that time. Word had drifted back of his being in Antioch, but it was uncertain. She had no way to get there anyway. Besides, what good would it do her to go? If he walked away before and would not come back, her chasing him would do no good. With him had gone all her support, but her body still cried for food. The landlord still called for rent. The merchants still demanded payment. He had not even had the decency to divorce her so she could remarry—not that any other man would likely want her, given the fact that she had produced no children. But was it her fault that she had not given him a son? How did he know the fault did not lie in him? But, of course, men were never at fault!

Look at her situation now—they had not even bothered to bring along the man with whom she had been found, although the law said that one was as guilty as the other. He had fled as soon as they had grabbed her, but they could have caught him easily enough if they had wanted to. It is difficult to run and dress at the same time! For that matter, she could have told them who he was, but what would that accomplish? He was a nobody. She wondered if it would have been different if the man with whom she had been found had been someone else—someone of importance whom she might embarrass by naming, someone rich enough or influential enough to hush it up or perhaps pay off the right person. She felt contempt for a system that arrested only one when two were so obviously guilty. How could one respect a law that punished the poor and let the rich walk away with a pittance of a fine or a mild slap on the fingers because they were considered too nice to really be criminals or sinners? Sometimes they received no penalty at all because they could buy the judge or hire a clever scribe to wring an excuse out of the dry pages of the books of the law. The amount of justice one received often seemed strangely proportionate to the amount of gold one could command. Or in this case, to what gender one happened to belong.

"Teacher," she heard one of them say, "this woman was taken in adultery, in the very act. Moses and the law say she should be stoned. What do you say?" A chill came over her at the word. Stoning! She didn't really think they would do that, especially after the conversation she had heard, but what if the crowd got angry enough and looked for something upon which to vent its anger? It might not be "official," but she would still be dead! She took what little comfort she could from the knowledge that they really only wanted to trap this man into something they could use to discredit him.

She raised her downcast eyes and saw that the teacher had dropped his gaze to the ground, probably when they named her sin she thought. He did not stare at her shame, paraded here before the temple and the crowds. A few had the decency to turn away as well, but others stared. Someone spit at her. That could have been the start of something ugly, but one of the Pharisees rebuked him and the spitter hurried off, afraid of the power of the men who stood around her. This was their show, and they wanted no one to spoil it by stirring up the crowd and perhaps taking action before their game was finished.

**74**

## WRITINGS IN THE DUST

Why did they hate him so much? What had he done to them? They had all the power and the position. They had the wealth and prestige. From what she had heard, he had no interest in either. Why then were they trying to discredit him? It was as if his disregard for all they thought so vital threatened to destroy the walls they had built around their lives. They could not stand to hear the truth that what they considered essential did not really matter. It was as if they were on trial, and they were trying to discredit the judge. That was it! His life and spirit was a judgment upon theirs. They could not bear it.

The teacher stooped down and began to trace in the dust. At first she thought that he was stalling, as if caught short by their challenge and hoping to think of something. The silence grew longer, and she felt a nervous stirring of the men around her who had brought her here. Perhaps they were feeling some embarrassment at the crudeness of their act—dragging her here to the temple, parading her sin this way.

Then she saw that the tracings were not meaningless at all. It was difficult to read them because they were upside down to her, but it was clearly writing that was there and not just lines in the dust. She blushed as she made out one word. "Adultery," she read. Was he writing her sentence in the dust? No, the next word was beneath the first, and there was another below that, like a list of some sort. "Anger" she saw. And then "Hatred . . . Jealousy . . . Greed."

## WRITINGS IN THE DUST

The accusers could not tolerate his silence any longer, and one of them shouted his question again. The teacher stopped his tracings and stood upright. In that moment his eyes burned with a strange fire, as if he knew full well their deception. When he spoke his voice was calm, yet it cut like a reaper's scythe. "He that is without sin among you, let him cast the first stone."

She gasped as she heard his words and half braced herself to feel the impact, even though she did not think they would stone her, for fear of the Romans, and because it was not really she whom they wanted but the teacher.

The teacher was writing in the dust again, and now her accusers had noticed the words. "Hypocrisy . . . False Witness . . . Murder." What was he doing? Was he suggesting that the accusers were guilty of some of those things? Was he implying that sin was sin, whatever form it took? She heard a sound behind her and saw a movement on her left. Two of the older Pharisees had turned away. Another followed, and then another. After him, another still, until at last they all were gone. Her attention went back to the dust to read again the list of words that he had written, but the ground was smooth now. As the last of her captors turned away, his hand had swept across the dust and rubbed them out.

She looked again at the dust where he had written the catalogue of sins, expecting to see at least hers still inscribed there, but that was gone as well. The dust was smooth, and, yes, clean—at least, as clean as dust can be.

## WRITINGS IN THE DUST

Smooth and unmarked, as if awaiting some new inscription to be written there, it was like some fresh piece of clay awaiting the potter's touch, like a canvas awaiting the artist's brush. Had dust ever looked so good? It was as if her life was spread out there, cleansed and whole and awaiting a new beginning. Would that it could be so easy!

The teacher had not looked at her while he was writing in the dust. Except for that one sharp glance at her accusers, he had spared them those piercing eyes that seemed to see right into a person's heart. He let them find their own guilt and accuse themselves. He let them walk away without staring at their shame and nakedness as they had stared at hers.

He looked at her now. His eyes fixed on hers, and she felt her bones become as water. She thought for a moment that she would fall. Then he spoke, "Woman, where are your accusers?" There was no surprise, no accusation in his voice, and yet she did not feel as if he did not care what she had done. She knew that he cared very much. She saw it in those eyes. She was not sure how she sensed it, but she did.

Suddenly what he had asked her sank in. Where were her accusers? They were gone! She had seen them leave. She looked around her now to make sure none had come back or remained where she had not seen them. The street was empty, save the traffic that was always there—the herdsman bringing his flock to market, the trader with his wares, the women with their water jars, people going about

77

their work. In that moment she knew what it was to have her life given back to her. No accusers meant no sentence of death for her this day. The stones would not crush out her life against the city wall. She knew then she was free.

"There are none, Lord," she whispered.

She faced now a worse accusation—worse than the contemptuous, self-righteous judgment of those who had walked away, worse than the staring eyes of the people who kept their distance, partly out of shame and partly out of not wanting to be involved. Now she was alone in the dust with him, the one whose own purity had saved her, alone with him and her own conscience. There was still his presence and still her own soul's accusation.

She knew the reason for her sin; knew the conditions that drove her to such a life to make her living; knew the injustice that crowded her where she did not want to be. But the reasons were not enough for her now. Excuses were not enough. She could not again be what she had been. She did not know what life would hold for her now, but she knew it would be different. Somehow there would be a way—a right way.

The teacher spoke again, and his voice swept through her soul like his hand across the dust, wiping out the tracings and the marks that had been there a moment before. "Neither do I condemn you. Go, and do not sin again."

She knew a kind of pity for her accusers in that moment. They walked away dragging their guilt with them. Hers was wiped away, blotted out in the dust of the street.

"Neither do I condemn you," he had said. That shook her to the center of her soul. Somehow, she sensed the purity of this man who stood before her. She had felt it when her accusers had brought her into this presence. It was as if it were a tangible thing, a force that radiated out from him. In fact, it was her sensing of that in him that made her really aware of her own sinfulness.

It was difficult for her to describe her feeling when she heard him say, "Neither do I condemn you." How can one describe what it means to be forgiven? There are no words for such a feeling, at least none that the lips can say or that ears can hear or that minds can understand. Hadn't she once heard a rabbi say that that was why the songs of the angels would be second best in heaven? The songs of the redeemed would have a sweeter sound, he had said. She knew now what he had meant. The angels have never known what it means to be forgiven.

She wasn't sure how she would face others after this day, but she knew that she could face herself and that, somehow, seemed the most important part. It would not be with a triumphant look, as if she had been accused unjustly and had been vindicated. Nor would it be the proud, self-righteous look of those who have found what they think is a sufficient excuse to justify what they have done. There is a difference in feeling forgiveness and trying to feel that one has never really sinned. Maybe the best analogy she could think of was *clean*. All the dirt and dust had been there, but now the dust was gone. Clean—the feeling one had after a refreshing bath on a hot and sticky day, the cool cleansing of the water as the dirt and dust washed away, the pleasant tingling of the skin that the rough toweling brought, the fragrant soothing of the oils and lotions—but it was more than the nerve-end sensations could offer. It was as if her *soul* had been washed clean.

Slowly she lifted her eyes from the dusty street. What else was it he had said? "Neither do I condemn you"— that had pierced her soul, but he had not stopped there. "Go and do not sin again."

He must know what she was going back to. There would be accusing glances, unforgiving, unforgetting neighbors and supposed friends, overtly evil ones who would assume that she would still be what she had been and try to prove their assumptions. The outwardly righteous ones would inwardly wait for her to fall again and would secretly suspect that she already had. And yet, he said, "Go and do not sin again." It was not a threat so much as a promise that he gave her, as if he were telling her to have that expectation of herself. It was as if he were expressing his own confidence that she would be able to do just that—to walk above the dust and dirt.

There would come a day when she would remember his writings in the dusty street. She would express her gratitude in a way that all the ages would recall, by washing the dust from his feet with her tears and anointing his feet with the precious ointment that one of her richer admirers had brought her long ago. But that was in the weeks to come, and she had no knowledge of that now, only the thrill of a life that was given back to her and the gratitude of a heart made whole again. A child of the dust had discovered that she was also a child of God. And the dust would never claim her again.

# CHAPTER 10

# A STUDY IN BLINDNESS

## John 9

Levi may not have been his name, but we will call him that. For more than thirty years he had felt the warmth of the sun on his eyelids, but he had never seen a sunrise or watched the sunlight sparkle on the water of the lake or gleam from the white stones of the temple or filter through the branches of the olive trees. He had smelled the anemonies on the hillsides and the smoke of sacrifice near the temple and the sheep and donkeys in the marketplace, but he had never seen the blossoms that marked the coming of spring or beheld the pageantry of worship in the temple court or watched the lambs kick their heels and run. He had felt the roughness of the stones of the temple wall and the smoothness of a baby's skin and the coarseness of new wool, but he had never gazed in awe at the towering pinnacle of the temple or beheld the wonder of a smile on a child's face or marveled at the patterns from a weaver's loom. He had tasted the sourness of the citrus, and he knew the sweetness of fresh bread, and he knew the salt of tears, but he had never marveled at the green skin of melons turning gold in the sun or watched the white loaves turning brown in the oven or seen the pain in another's eyes. Levi had tasted and felt and touched, but he had never seen. Levi was blind. He had been blind from the day of his birth.

His family had taught him to beg at the best places for the simple reason that there was no other way for them to manage. There were days when he earned more than his father did working—but not many. And he would much rather have been able to work.

This day had not started out much differently than any other. He was at his place near the temple—a good place because worshipers going to or coming from the Holy Place were usually more generous than persons in other parts of the city. Whether it was from guilt or gratitude, he couldn't really tell. All he knew was that the coins were a bit more frequent and often larger.

He heard a murmur run through the crowd. With the extra sense of hearing that the blind develop, he recognized that some interesting or prominent person was passing by. He soon knew that it was a teacher, because someone called him that, but he felt a shock go through his system as he heard the rest of what the disciple asked his teacher: "Rabbi, who sinned—this man or his parents— that he was born blind?" Levi felt a wave of resentment at the question. How could his sin have anything to do with it? He had been *born* blind! Did they think because he moved in his mother's womb on the Sabbath that he was guilty of breaking the Sabbath? As for his parents, he had long since stopped believing in the perfection of parents. They were better than many, he was sure, since they hadn't abandoned him in the streets someplace or thrown him over the wall for the jackals to eat, but he didn't question that they had sinned. Blind as he was, he could even name a few of those sins!

But what had that to do with his blindness? Why should he be punished for something they might have done? Sure, his blindness had been a burden to them, especially in the early years, but somehow the idea that God was punishing his parents by afflicting him for something his parents had done didn't make much sense. Certainly it was the kind of question that only one who wasn't suffering could ever ask! If God were like *that,* he thought, what chance do we have? We might serve God, lest something worse happen to us, he supposed, but to talk about *loving* God made no sense at all. He had about decided that such questions revealed that there was more than one kind of blindness. Just then he heard another voice answering the disciple's question.

"It was not that this man sinned, or his parents. . . ." Well, now! There was a refreshing view! He wasn't sure he wanted to push that affirmation of innocence too far, in view of his previous reflection about his parents and his knowledge of himself. But at least there was someone around who saw things a bit more clearly than that first questioner!

## WRITINGS IN THE DUST

He heard a kind authority in the voice as it went on. "But that the works of God might be made manifest in him...." Now what did he mean by that? Was he implying that he had been left blind for more than thirty years so God could prove something? Not a whole lot better than the other idea, was his first thought. Convenient enough for God, he supposed, but pretty hard on him. Thirty years might not seem all that long to God, but it was all the time he had had. But the voice went on—words about "doing the work of one who had sent him while it was day" and "being the light of the world."

He heard the sound of spitting then and cringed a bit before he realized that it was not at him. Then he felt a moisture applied to his eyes, and he knew the stranger had made clay from the dust and spittle and put it on his eyes. There was a coolness to it and a kindness in the touch that came through his darkness. The same voice spoke again, "Go wash in the pool of Siloam."

Almost without knowing why, he struggled to his feet and started off. It was not a short journey, especially for a blind man—all the way out the gates of the city and down the finger ridge running southeast towards the older part of David's city. He had been there before, however, and with the incredible ability to go by sound and touch that came from thirty years' training in the strictest school—necessity— he made his journey.

How could he ever describe that walk? An hour that seemed a lifetime! Hope, fear, chagrin, bitterness—many emotions swept through him, but always he came back to hope. He kept thinking of the words that the teacher had said about his blindness. Depending on how one placed the pauses and the inflections, it seemed as if he could be saying that he, the teacher, was showing his disciples what the will of God *really* was by giving Levi his sight!

If only that could be true! There was one who saw clearly enough what a loving God must *intend* whatever the whys and wherefores that brought blindness into the world, when no one's choice and actions had any part in it.

He had reached the pool. A few friendly helpers had made it somewhat easier, although some had laughed at the mud on his face and made unkind remarks about not needing to be filthy as well as blind. But he didn't care. He was used to verbal abuses by this time. Besides, he still walked in hope.

He paused a moment by the pool. This was the moment of truth. He had come this far in hope. Now he faced the possibility that hope would be dashed with a far colder water than the pool held for his body. Is it better to go on hoping for some future healing than to have hope so tested and shattered? Could he go back to his begging bowl if he came out of the water? For that matter, what would he do for a living if he *did* receive his sight? Was the teacher playing a cruel trick on him? Had they followed along at some distance to laugh at him when he went through with his charade? It sounded cruel, but he had been tricked and abused before, and hope such as this was no matter to trifle with. Whoever talked about hope in glib terms never had to put it to the test, he decided.

He recalled the kind authority of that voice. "As long as I am in the world, I am the light of the world. . . . I must work the works of him that sent me." And it was as if Levi could feel again the touch of those fingers on his eyes. He suddenly realized that there had been no promises made at all! Nothing was said about healing him. Not really. It was all implied in what happened. The conversations, the applications of the spittle mud, the command to go wash—he could stand the debate no longer. Scooping water from the pool, he washed the mud from his eyes. . . .

He could see!

He had often asked one of his friends to describe a sunset or some other beautiful sight to him when he heard them discussing it. He had often been told, "I don't know how to describe it because you've never had anything with which to compare it." Now he knew what they meant because he knew that he could never describe what it is like to receive your sight to someone who had never been without it! How do you describe the glory of light and color and brightness and shadows to those who have never known their absence?

The journey back seemed to take forever. He wanted to run, to share the news, to see (to *see*!) the One who had healed him, but there was much else to see! His own hands and feet, his reflection in the pool, the blue of the sky, the green of the trees, the whiteness of the city walls, the colors of the clothing and the faces of the people who had brushed by him for thirty years, the shaggy coats of sheep and goats that he had touched and heard and smelled, the flashing feet of children running, the dogs that barked, the chickens scurrying away in the dust. But finally he made it back to the temple area.

The teacher was gone, but Levi's arrival caused plenty of excitement. He was known there because he had sat at the same place so frequently and some began to call to others to come and see this wonder. Some said he wasn't the same man. (Were *they* blind? Of course he was the same man! And he told them so.)

He soon found that receiving sight was not all that easy. He suddenly found himself before the Pharisees, that awesome group who held much power over the lives of his people. They wanted to know who healed him and how and what he thought about his healing and who he thought his healer was.

Suddenly he found himself in the midst of more controversy than he had ever known in his sightless days, and again he became aware that there were more kinds of blindness than he had ever realized. He had encountered the blind fatalism of some who asked questions similar to the disciples who had started his experiences that day, but here was such blindness as he had never seen before! (He smiled to himself at that. Of course, he hadn't *seen* it before.) Here was blindness that could look on good and call it evil. "He healed on the Sabbath," some of them complained. "He is not from God because he is a sinner," others added.

They called in his parents, not believing his testimony or their own eyes since most of them had passed him by often enough in the days that he had sat there begging. But maybe they didn't "see" him then. He was rapidly learning that having eyes and seeing were not the same thing.

Finally he could stand their interrogation no longer and in a sharp outburst, when they asked him to repeat his story, he quipped: "I have told you several times. Why do you want to hear it again? Do you want him to heal you?" He knew as soon as he said it that it was too much. In quick anger, they rebuked him and cast him out of the temple—not simply bodily but in an act of excommunication that cut him off from the ritual and worship of his people.

It was a solemn thing, and he regretted his outburst. But he could stand their blindness no longer. The only good that came from it was to bring the teacher back to him. Someone had told the teacher what had happened and he had returned. Levi recognized the voice when he asked, "Do you believe in the Son of man?"

Never versed in the finer points of theology, he had replied, "Who is he, sir, that I may believe in him?"

There was a smile in those eyes when the teacher

replied, "You have *seen* him—and it is he who speaks to you."

And looking into that face, Levi answered, "Lord, I believe." Then he truly saw! And that night before he finally closed his eyes to shut out the light, he said a prayer for those who had eyes but still could not see.

# CHAPTER 11

# A MAN AND HIS MEMORIES

Luke 22: 31-62; John 13: 1-11

In a far corner of the courtyard, a group of workmen were hewing rough beams of wood. Two of them were lashing a smaller piece across a heavier, providing a mute but vivid testimony of the object of their labors. Near the center of the enclosure a group of soldiers gathered about the remains of a fire, stamping the chill of the night from their feet and drinking from a wine jug that was being passed around the circle.

"Take a drink, lad," an older one urged a younger member of the group. "You'll need it before this day's work is done."

"How many is it this time?" another asked.

"Two, at least," the senior officer replied. "And from the looks on the faces of the mob I saw in Pilate's court, I'd say probably three."

A rooster flew down from the wall. He had announced

the time of sunrise, and had remained on the wall until he was certain that the sun was answering his summons. Now that the sun had appeared, a red ball burning through the eastern sky, he strutted over to his harem, scratching for breakfast in the dust.

On the other side of the wall, a man stood beside a gnarled tree. One rough hand clutched a rough branch so tightly that the knuckles stood out, white. He was a big man. His broad, heavy shoulders spoke of a strength that came from hard work. Now those shoulders shook with sobs. Simon Peter was weeping.

The crowing of the cock still rang in his ears, sending other echoes ringing through the chambers of his soul. "Before the cock crows, you will deny me three times."

The remembrance of those words burned like a searing iron. How could he have done it? "Jesus of Nazareth? I never knew the man!" Not once, but three times he had said it! If a man could only live a few minutes of his life over again—no, he decided. He would need more than a few minutes. He would cast the entire night out of his life forever if he could.

It had started on the journey from Bethany to Jerusalem. James and John had started it with their eternal bickering about who would sit on Jesus' right hand and who on his left when he came into his kingdom. Matthew and Thomas had joined in and soon the whole group was involved in a controversy over who among them was the greatest. The dispute had raged almost the entire time the short walk required. He had remained silent as long as he could.

Finally he had turned to John and demanded, "Why do you argue over whose place it will be? Didn't you hear the Master's words in Caesarea Philippi? 'Thou art Peter, and on this rock I will build my church, and the gates of hell shall not prevail against it'?"

John had been horrified. "Peter, you know he was referring to the rock of your testimony concerning who he was, not you yourself!"

His brother Andrew had chimed in then, "Besides, you would never even have met the Master if I hadn't persuaded you to come and see him."

A quick reply had been on his lips, but suddenly they were at the home of John Mark, where they had been offered an upper room in which to celebrate the Passover. The argument subsided to sullen muttering as they climbed the outside stairway. Jesus had never looked back. Perhaps he had not heard what they were saying.

A basin of water and a towel had been placed inside the door, awaiting the ministries of a servant who would remove their sandals and wash the dust from their feet. It was a common courtesy, performed in the most humble homes. The disciples took turns performing the task when there was no regular household servant assigned to do it. There would be no servant this evening. The Master had expressly requested that the group not be disturbed. Something seemed to be weighing on his mind, and he wanted to talk to his closest followers alone.

Peter had looked at the basin and towel a second time. He suddenly remembered that it was his turn tonight. He had hesitated a second, then walked on to the low couches which surrounded the table. He was in no mood to wash John's feet or the feet of any of the others, for that matter, not after the argument of the evening. It would be more fitting if one of them would wash *his* feet.

An awkward silence had followed, as they all waited for someone to act as servant and wash their feet before the meal began. The argument had affected each of them the same way. No one cared to compromise his position by stooping to the task of a servant. Finally someone at the table moved. With a start, Simon Peter saw that it was Jesus. With mounting horror, he had watched his leader walk toward the basin and towel. Without a word, he laid aside his outer robe and wrapped the towel about his waist in the manner of a servant. No one moved. They hardly breathed as, one by one, he knelt before them, loosened the strap of the sandal and bathed their feet in water, then dried them on the towel. Each man's eyes were fixed upon his feet and the strong hand that bathed them. Each man waited for him to speak some word or look into their eyes that they might speak and break the spell of silence that gripped the room. But he spoke no word. And he did not look up. He seemed to be doing it—as a servant would, with perhaps a touch of sadness in his eyes. Each man knew that he had failed him again.

But Simon Peter could not be still. His own voice had

sounded strange to him as it shattered the silence. "Lord, you—to wash my feet! It shall never be!"

The rebuke had come quickly then. "Unless I wash you, you will not share my fellowship."

In hasty penitence, Simon remembered how he had blurted out, "Then not my feet only, but also my hands and my head."

He sighed as he recalled it. Couldn't he ever learn to keep still? Washing the feet had been enough for the others. The Master had gently reminded him that he knew what he was doing without Simon's suggestions. "A man who has come from the bath need only wash his feet and he is altogether clean," he had said.

Peter had vowed then that there would be no more arguments about who was the greatest among them. The words of Jesus had hardly been necessary when they came. They only verbalized what he had already said more vividly than any spoken message. "The servant is not above the Master. As I have washed your feet, so should you wash one another's feet. He that would be great among you, let him be your servant."

It had been then that Jesus had made his startling prophecy. "One of you shall betray me," he announced. Anxious eyes turned from one to another. After the experience they had just had, each one searched his own soul. Some were heard to whisper, "Lord, is it I?" Jesus had identified his betrayer, but the little band was too shocked to recognize the disclosure.

## WRITINGS IN THE DUST

Peter straightened beside the tree. His hand slipped to the hilt of his short sword. If he had known then what he knew now, there would have been no betrayal—then his hand fell away. Who was he to execute judgment? Was Judas' betrayal really any worse than his own? Three times he had said it: "I never knew the man." "I never knew the man." "I never knew the man."

Finally his thoughts went back to the upper room again. How brave he had sounded then! Jesus had told them plainly that he was shortly going to leave them. Moreover, he added, "Where I am going, you cannot come."

Immediately Peter had answered, "Lord, why can I not follow you? I would lay down my life for you." Brave words then—foolish words now. He could still feel the weight of the Master's eyes and his answer, "Peter, before the cock crows to announce sunrise, you will deny me three times." How absurd the words had sounded then. How they burned into his soul now.

Peter admitted to himself: I have repented for some of my hasty actions, it is true. In my anger, I sliced off the ear of one of the soldiers who came to arrest Jesus, and Jesus restored it on the spot. It was probably my haste that saved the fellow's life, for that matter. I was aiming for his head, but in my hurry . . . . But, was it tolerable that the finest soul the world had ever known should be taken away without a word of resistance? He chose that way, and I understand it now. To accept death for one's friends and loved ones is sometimes not as easy as accepting one's own death. I would have died for him, but to let him die for me—that was an even harder thing to do! You know!

Suddenly a new light began to creep into Peter's face. He remembered something else Jesus had said. How had he phrased it?

> Simon, Satan has demanded to have you, that he might sift you like wheat; but I have prayed for you that your faith may not fail; and when you have come to yourself, lend strength to your brothers.
>
> —Luke 22:31-32, AP

Even before his sin had been committed, forgiveness had been ready for him. Could he do less than accept it now? He walked back to the gate of the courtyard. The soldiers were making ready to leave. The cross makers had completed their work. The three crosses leaned against the wall, waiting for the condemned men to walk under them and carry them to the appointed place. A shudder wracked Peter's body. He had seen a crucifixion before. He could recall now the broken, bleeding figure hanging there. It had been a terrible death—the broken body, the bleeding face and side.

Then, like a blaze of summer lightning, the other event of that evening flashed before him. It was while they were eating. The Master had taken a piece of bread and broken it and passed it among them. "This is my body," he had said, "broken for you." Likewise, after supper he had taken the cup and given it to them, this time saying, "This is the new covenant of my blood which is poured out for many for the forgiveness of sins.'' It hadn't made much sense at the time, but now. . . .

Peter looked toward the rising sun. Soon the Passover lambs would be slain in the temple courts, sacrifice provided for the appeasement of God's wrath, and soon the Lamb of God would die upon a cross, the sacrifice that God had provided to demonstrate his love.

Peter squared his shoulders and started off to look for John. Tears of sorrow and repentance still rolled down his cheeks, but mingled with them now were tears of the beginning of an understanding, an understanding that would grow until the kingdoms of this world became the kingdom of our Lord and Jesus Christ.

# CHAPTER 12

# CONVERSATION BY THE SEA

John 21:1-19

Everything was waiting for the sun.

The scraps of canvas tied to the masts of the fishing boats to detect the wind hung listlessly in the morning air. The harsh cry of a sea gull pierced the hush of dawn. In the silence that heralded the sunrise, one could hear the whisper of its wings as it flapped along, searching for the invisible current of air that had temporarily disappeared.

Even the lake was still. The waves made not even the gentlest lapping against the rocks along the shoreline. It was as though the world had no energy to spare to move the waves or stir the canvas or support a sea gull too lazy to flap a wing, but needed all its strength to concentrate on the sunrise.

Finally the horizon relinquished the sun, and forth it came, red and flushed from its efforts, bathing the world in redness. Slowly, the exertion over, winning again the daily battle with the skyline, the flush subsided and energy returned again to the rest of the world. The bits of canvas fluttered. The waves increased their lapping, and at last the sea gull found its breeze. Morning had come to the sea of Tiberias.

The flatness of the early light reflected the surroundings like a picture etched in steel. A single fishing boat floated a short distance offshore. There was considerable activity on the boat. No one stopped to observe the beauty. These men had seen many sunrises, and this morning their minds were on other things. They were fishing—in fact, they had been fishing all night, and their bodies were weary from the repeated throwing and pulling of their nets. Empty nets are more tiring than nets with fish in them, and empty the nets had been, all night long.

Once or twice Simon Peter had wondered what had ever prompted him to suggest they go fishing. His mind had not been on fish. Still, a man must do something. Sitting around wondering what the events of the previous days were going to mean was too much for a man more used to action than to meditation. He had felt a need to feel again the pull of a heavy net in his hands, to hear the slap of wind in canvas, to feel the breeze in his face, and to smell the sea. And so he said, "I go a fishing" (John 21:3).

As soon as he had suggested fishing, he had a crew. Others seemed to feel the same restlessness. Six of his fellow disciples had replied, "We will go with you." All night long they had toiled with the nets, but every cast came back the same. All the favorite sites were worked over until their arms ached, but sunrise found their vessel as empty as the previous nightfall had left it.

At first, the activity itself had brought a welcome relief to their weary minds, crammed as they were with wondrous and mysterious things. There had been a midnight arrest, followed by a horrible crucifixion, and then that despairing sabbath when they could not even go to the grave to anoint the body. Then they had the earth-shaking discovery that the tomb was empty, and finally the unforgettable moment when Jesus had appeared in their midst— not once but twice. He appeared once when Thomas was not with them and again when he was, as if to silence a doubter's question. Frankly, Simon was as thankful as Thomas for the second appearance, for he had begun to doubt his own sanity, even though nine others had verified his own experience. A resurrection was not something one took lightly.

The first half of the night had passed without a thought of all of that. Their minds were so tired from trying to think of what it meant that the physical efforts of casting and pulling their nets had been more refreshing than sleep. Gradually, however, the thoughts returned. Fishing gives one a chance to think in a different way, and by sunrise Peter's mind was as busy as his arms.

What was it the Master had said when Peter first met him at his father's fishing boat? ''Come after me and I will make you fishers of men!'' (see Matt. 4:19). What could

*103*

that mean now? Was the news of the resurrection the net they were to cast into the sea of humanity?

Peter's thoughts were interrupted by a hail from the shore. "Have you caught any fish?" Looking up, he saw a solitary figure standing on the beach.

One of the other men replied, "No luck. Just empty nets and sore backs."

"Cast your net on the right side of the boat, and you will catch some," the figure called. The fishermen looked at one another for a moment, shrugged, and did as the man suggested. An observer on the shore could often see a school of feeding fish more clearly than the fishermen because of the angle of the light. As soon as they tightened their ropes, Peter knew they had a haul. The nets were strained to the breaking point, but somehow they held.

John, who was standing near Peter, looked again at the figure on the shore and whispered, "It's the Master."

Peter looked again himself, then leaped over the side of the boat, and waded the hundred yards to shore before the others could bring the boat to land.

A fish was broiling on a bed of coals when he got there, and Jesus invited all of them to share the bread and meat. But Peter could not keep his eyes off of Jesus. Three times now he had appeared among them. He looked different, but yet not different. Sometimes he looked the same as he had before that day on Calvary, and sometimes it was as though he were another person. Yet the two were becoming one in his mind, and it was getting harder and harder

*104*

to sort out Jesus of Nazareth and the Resurrected Christ. Well, he thought, I suppose death and resurrection would be expected to make some changes in a man. Peter shuddered a little at the thought and took a piece of bread.

Then Jesus spoke to him. "Simon, son of John, do you love me more than these?"

A shock went through Peter's frame, but almost automatically he answered, "Yes, Lord, you know that I love you." Even as he said the words, he had a fleeting vision of another scene with a fire and a group of people standing about warming themselves in the light of dawn. He had been asked about his relationship with Jesus then, too, and he had replied that he never even knew the man.

What is it about a person that makes him or her so fickle to circumstance? Here he was answering as quickly in the affirmative concerning a relationship that just a few days before he had denied with equal haste. In neither instance was it an answer he had really thought about ahead of time, just the surface reaction to the emotions of the situation. "Yes, Lord, you know I love you" . . . "I never even knew the man." Just words. It took no more breath to say one phrase than to say the other.

How easy it is to tune our conversation to the crowd we are with, to say what we think they want to hear or what we think will be the safest thing at the moment. How glib the tongue can be! How revealing and yet how concealing! Truth and falsehood from the same source—who has the wisdom to know when it is one and when the other? Words

**105**

themselves are not true or false, good or bad. They are only instruments by which people express themselves. It is we who are true or false, not the words we say.

Almost as if Jesus had read his thoughts, he asked Peter again, "Simon, son of John, *do* you love me?"

There was less haste this time in Simon's answer. His words were the same as before, just as the question was the same, but they came from a different level of his being. His glance took in the fishing boat, pulled up from the lake, the pile of nets on its deck, the great catch of fish. He looked at his comrades gathered around the fire. In that moment, he felt all the pull of the old way of life. Did he love Jesus more than these? It was a way of life that had attractions for him in spite of all its sweat and effort. Fishing was a respectable occupation. In good season, it provided a comfortable living. One could usually get by, even in bad times. He knew that his answer had something to do with all this. The old way might still be a part of him, as far as a way of making a living was concerned, but it could never be the same again—not if he *meant* what he said. He was primarily a fisher of men now, only incidently a fisher of fish.

That is not a decision one makes lightly. If a person thinks it is, that one had better not make it yet. Let each person ponder his or her own predisposition to cherish the old ways and the reluctance to take up the new.

If one could leave the old way entirely, go into a temple and live there like the high priest, it might be easier. But to stay in the old occupation with a new spirit and to make that spirit permeate every action and every decision, *to make the old life new,* that was another thing entirely. He might often be surrounded by the same companions, doing the same things, meeting the same frustrations, facing the same decisions and choices that he had faced before, but there would be a new factor involved. Love wasn't just a word you said. Love was something that affected your whole life.

Thoughts can go very quickly sometimes. They can cover a lifetime in a few seconds, or at least the things about a life that mean very much. All this passed through Peter's mind as he heard himself say, with some feeling this time, "Yes, Lord, you know that I love you."

There was a moment before Jesus spoke again, and in that silence Peter was aware of the buzz of other conversation around them. Overhead the gulls were circling, hoping the fishermen would go away and leave the pile of fish to rot on the beach so they could gorge themselves too full to fly. With the changing angle of the sun, the softer light was giving way to the brilliance that marked full morning, and the close-lying hills that encompassed the lake shown now in detail instead of silhouette.

Peter could hardly believe his ears when he heard Jesus speak again. "Simon, son of John, do you love me?"

A feeling of despair swept over Peter. Didn't the Master believe him? Didn't Jesus think he had thought before he spoke—at least the second time? Didn't he know . . . then

**107**

Simon remembered the questioning beside the other fire. He had answered three times then also. Three times he had denied that he was a follower of the man he was now professing to love. Was Jesus asking him to affirm his love three times in order to atone for those three denials?

Somehow that didn't seem quite motive enough. It seemed too easy an out. After all, there was nothing at stake in professing to be a disciple of Jesus here. Everyone else at this place would say the same thing. The only way he could demonstrate his change of heart from that night would be to make his witness where it meant something, where it wasn't just the expected thing.

One would have thought it would be impossible to ring so many changes on so simple a question as ''Do you love me?'' but there were many new thoughts running through Simon's mind as he prepared to answer for a third time.

Was it really Christ that he loved, or was it the respectability of being a part of the Miracle Worker's inner circle? Was it really love that he felt or was it merely admiration or respect? Did what he felt involve commitment and dedication, or was it fickle emotionalism? Was it something that would hold firm if another test, like the one that he had failed a few nights before, should arise?

Simon thought a moment. He had learned his lesson. The gracious forgiveness he had felt following his denial, when Jesus had walked by and turned his eyes upon him, had made him stronger. He could affirm his love now, not only before Jesus and the little band of disciples, but before the whole world.

There would come a day when he would again recall that night and his denial. When they prepared to crucify him, he would remember and say, "Not as he died; but with my head downward. I am not worthy to share his manner of death." And his executioners would honor his request. But that was in the future, and this was now. Besides, one does not have to feel worthy in order to love. That very sense of unworthiness would only serve to deepen his devotion.

So, for the third time Simon answered the same question with the same words. And yet, it wasn't the same. It wasn't the same question, and it wasn't the same answer. Each question had probed deeper into his heart and each answer had revealed his heart more fully, not only to his Lord but to himself.

"Lord, you know everything. You know that I love you."

And this time, Simon knew it, too.